DIVINE JUSTICE

THE
DIANNE ALEXANDER
STORY

THE ONLY SURVIVOR
OF THE DERRICK
TODD LEE MURDERS

God Bless !.
Tanya

DIVINE JUSTICE

Dianne Alexander

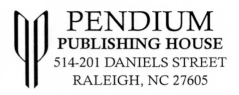

PENDIUM
PUBLISHING HOUSE
514-201 DANIELS STREET
RALEIGH, NC 27605

For information, please visit our Web site at
www.pendiumpublishing.com

PENDIUM Publishing and its logo
are registered trademarks.

Divine Justice:
The Dianne Alexander Story
By Dianne Alexander

Unless otherwise indicated, all bible quotations are taken from the
KJV and Century versions of the bible.

PUBLISHER'S NOTE

Table of Contents

Dedication

This book is dedicated to my Heavenly Father whom I sincerely love, and who has inspired me to write this book. All glory and honor belongs to Him.

In Memory of

Geralyn DeSoto, Gina Green, Pam Kinamore, Trinisha Dene' Colomb, Charlotte Murray Pace, Carrie Yoder, Connie Warner, and Randi Mebruer.

My heart goes out to the families of these women and my prayers are continuously with them.

I also pray for Derrick Todd Lee's mom. She is not responsible for his actions.

Acknowledgements

To the one who saved my soul and delivered me from the power of darkness; my Lord and Savior, Jesus Christ, son of the living God . . . I give you honor and praise.

I would like to give special thanks to Oliver, my former husband, and my children and stepchildren, Tamika, Reginald, Djuanas, Herman, Tiffany, Keaha, and Olivia. To my mom, Doris and my dad, the late Herman Davis, I thank God for you. You were awesome parents; full of love for one another as well as your children. To my siblings, Wanda, Dorothy, Terry, Janet, Darrell, and my sister, Judy, who has gone to be with the Lord—thank you for your love and support. To my nieces, nephews, relatives, and friends, thank you for your prayers and encouragement.

I would especially like to acknowledge Linda,

Wanda and Ernest, my Mom, and Dorothy and Eric for allowing Oliver and I to stay in their homes during out trying times. I also acknowledge Keith and my neice, Kesha (who has also gone to be with the Lord), for taking Herman under their wings in his time of need.

Special thanks to my friend and editor, Nedra Epps, who gladly accepted the call from God to assist me with this assignment.

To Debra Milson, my professional and spiritual counselor, who became a friend to both Oliver and I. God could not have chosen a better person to help me overcome my emotional dilemmas.

To All of St Martin Parish Law Enforcement— thanks for your hard work in bringing Derrick Todd Lee to justice.

Lt. Rena Williams, my dearest friend and victim's advocate—thanks Rena, for your emotional support and sticking by my side through the darkest time in my life.

I'd like to acknowledge Captain Audrey Thibodeaux, Director of Victim's Services for her support and for being a part of my journey.

Detective Arthur Boyd, I commend you for your diligence in finding my attacker. You worked tirelessly on my case and never gave up until all the pieces of the puzzle came together. I thank God for using you, and I thank you for accepting the assignment.

To Detective Marcus Guidry, thank you for assisting in the investigation.

Chester Cedars, Assistant District Attorney for the 16th Judicial District Attorney's Office who prosecuted Derrick Todd Lee—I also thank you and your staff for helping me in many areas of my life during this journey.

I would also like to thank Acadiana Crime Lab for discovering Derrick Todd Lee's DNA Marker from his sweat that fell onto the collar of my dress, which was covered by my blood due to the blunt force trauma to my head. Awesome job!!!

To East and West Baton Rouge Parish Law Enforcement and to everyone who has been a part of my life during this journey . . . thank you.

I thank God for the Victim's Crime Reparation Board for making themselves available to assist me in my time of need.

To Sterling and Yvonne Dorsey Colomb and, and the Colomb family—thank you for your generosity and emotional support.

To Greg Mouton and Bob Foti—thank you for your loving encouragement.

To Mike and Gail Dartez, as well as the late Lorraine Sterling and her family, thank you for your part in making this project a reality.

To Patricia Calais, my friend and admitting nurse on the Oncology Unit and Linda Benjamin—a very special nurse assigned to me on the Othro-Neuro Unit at the time of my incident—thank you for your compassionate care.

To the 911 operator, paramedics, and the staff of Lafayette General Medical Center—thank you for your helping hands and caring hearts.

To Dr. Thomas Bertuccini and Dr. Terry Cromwell—I thank God for giving you the knowledge and wisdom as you cared for me.

To Pastor Ken, his wife, Mary, his mother Renee, and my former church family, Destiny of Faith, thank you for keeping me covered in prayer at a most crucial time in my life.

To Bishop Lloyd and The Spirit of Liberty family, I appreciate you. This is the place where I began to grow and mature in God. An evening service called "Tearing down the Walls in Your Life" changed my life dramatically. This is where my journey began.

To my dear, sweet Pastor and friend, Eloyce Benoit and Living Word Christian Fellowship Church, I am so grateful to God for allowing me to fellowship with you and be a part of your congregation. You are an awesome blessing in my life.

To the families of the women that this book is in memory of, thank you for supporting me when I went to trial. Last but not least, I want to praise God for my spiritual prayer partner; the late Nicole Gant Reed, who was an awesome inspiration to me. I thank God for sending me another prayer partner, Karen Dean. Thank you for answering the call.

May the Blessings of God be upon each and every one of you. Please forgive me if you were not mentioned in the acknowledgements. It was not intentional. I love and appreciate everyone who has been a part of my journey.

Preface

O n July 9, 2002 I was viciously attacked in my home. I didn't know at the time that the attacker was serial killer, Derrick Todd Lee, or that I would be the only survivor of six known attacks upon women, by this man. That event had a significant impact upon my life and the way I view things. However, the attack was not the beginning, nor was it the end of my life.

As a result of this event, the Lord spoke to my heart to write this book. In 2007 He said, "Tell your story". I said, "Lord, what are you talking about? What story?" He brought back to my remembrance that I had not spoken to the media regarding my attack. Prior to the trial, several media sources called, including Inside Edition, stating they were interested in my story. The D.A. advised me not to speak to the media due to the fact that the trial was pending. I politely rejected their request.

The Lord said the story was contained within me for an appointed time, and no one could tell it the way I could, because this was my experience. He took me to Micah 6:1 in the New Century Version Bible which said, "Now hear what the Lord says; Get up; plead your case in front of the mountains; let the hills hear your story". In other words, it was time for my story to go forth so I can tell others of how God was undoubtedly present in the midst of my ordeal. The confirmation of His Word bore witness with my spirit.

Immediately I knew I must do as He commanded. My greatest fear is disobedience to God. I've been there many times before and the repercussions are not so good. Although He loves us and forgives us when we sincerely ask Him, we tend to have a difficult time forgiving ourselves for offending Him. I was willing to do anything for God.

I struggled with such uneasiness within myself about writing this book. I didn't have the slightest clue of where to begin. The Holy Spirit continuously tugged at me until I gave up my will for the will of

God. I realized that I am only a vessel, and all I had to do was say "yes", then God would do the rest.

The bible clearly states that obedience is far better than sacrifice (1Samuel 15:22 New Living Translation). This assignment was bigger than me; but with God, all things are possible (Mark 10:22 KJV). I asked The Holy Spirit to lead and guide me as I went forward in writing this book.

As I pressed on with the task that was required of me, I continued to ask God for a title to the book. Finally, the Lord gave it to me in an open vision. One day I was driving on I-49 going to visit my son, Reginald, who was serving time in Cottonport, La. While in my car, I looked up in the sky, and I saw something similar to a pebble falling from afar. As it got closer, the object became larger until finally I recognized the word "*justice*"; and it literally hit me like a tap on my forehead. This may sound silly or foolish to some, but God has chosen the foolish things of the world to confound the wise (1Corinthians 1:27 KJV.). God is a spirit, and the only reason I saw this vision is because He opened my spiritual eyes and allowed me to see it.

At that point I realized the Lord had given me the title of the book. It was just amazing the way He did it. I was overwhelmed with joy and rejoiced within my spirit. The Lord loves us so much that He actually takes the time to answer when we call upon Him.

My story is about trusting God in the midst of any situation that you find yourself, even when you don't understand what's going on. One moment, everything in our little world seems to fall in place and all is well. Then suddenly, when we least expect it, our little world as we know it, is turned upside down. This is what happened to me when I answered the door to assist someone who claimed to be lost. My life was on the line and I didn't even know it.

Sometimes the circumstances we go through in life may seem to be more than we can bear. But, God promised He would be with us until the end of time if we put our in trust Him. He also said that He wouldn't put more on us than we can bear. He created us, so He knows whether or not we can handle the test or trial that comes our way. I believe Him with my whole heart and my entire being. I pray that my story will inspire you to see the goodness of Our Heavenly Father.

God is faithful in everything He does. If Derrick Todd Lee had taken my life . . . . my spirit and soul belonged to God . . . that, he could not destroy.

GOD is just. No one renders justice like He does. As human beings, we try to figure out why certain things happen to us and what we have done to deserve such unpleasant events in our lives. As difficult as it may seem, we must trust God. I know about trusting Him in the worst of times; especially, when a situation appears to be so unbearable, that you wake up in the morning feeling numb to reality. You're hoping that this thing that has come to change your world is a dream you can wake up from. Suddenly you come to yourself and realize that this horrible situation actually happened. Your life is changed forever. You can't go back to the way things were, and you don't know how to move on.

For 46 years, I lived a normal life. I had my own dreams and desires prior to this event and had even begun to see some of them come to pass. From childhood to adulthood, I have come through many challenges, but God has always been faithful through each of them.

There were some things that happened to me prior to the attack as well as since the attack that have truly shaped my life and made me the person that I am today. I am inspired to tell you about the One who is the reason I survived that attack and why I am here today to tell my story. God deserves so much more attention than me or the man who attacked me. My desire is for you to know Him the way I have come to know Him. I never would have imagined that something that horrible could happen to me or that I would be the only one to survive it.

God left me here for a reason. Through this book, perhaps you will understand why I am still here. But I hope you will also understand, with all that you've been through, why you are still here as well. We will explore this together.

Introduction

My Life Before

I grew up in a small town called Breaux Bridge, Louisiana. My dad was a hard worker; my mother, a housewife. I was the second child of seven children. My siblings and I had a normal childhood. I dropped out of school after completing the tenth grade, got married two years later, and had two children from this marriage—Tamika and Reginald.

After three years of marriage, my first husband and I separated. We were divorced seven years later. Shortly after my divorce, I married Oliver Alexander. We have two sons—Djuanas and Herman. I also have three stepdaughters—Tiffany, Keaha, and Olivia. The girls lived within the city limits of Breaux Bridge and would visit us on different occasions.

Tiffany and Keaha lived with their grandmother, and Olivia lived with her mother. Oliver, my four children and I, lived in a country setting outside the city limits of Breaux Bridge. The area was recognized as Poche Bridge/Cecilia area. I enjoyed living there because it was family oriented. We resided there for approximately twelve years. Prior to moving to Cecilia, I attended adult education classes and received my GED. Later on, I decided to attend nursing school.

My desire to become a nurse started while I was attending junior high. A few of my friends and I were discussing what we wanted to become once we graduated. I had two desires. One was to become an airline stewardess, and the second was to become a nurse. I enjoy traveling and also caring for others. The Lord blessed me so that I was able to do some traveling (although I never became an airline stewardess). Instead, I decided to pursue a nursing career. In Psalms 37:4 God said, "Delight yourself also in the Lord, and He shall give you the desires of your heart."

My journey as a nursing student began in 1992. I was 32-years-old. I figured that if I was still able to function mentally, why not go for it? The journey wasn't as easy as I thought it would be. I attended many different schools trying to achieve my degree in a hurry. The hardest lesson I had to learn wasn't my college courses; it was patience. I learned patience through endurance of test and trials. The Bible says the trying of our faith brings forth patience (James 1:3). This could not be more true. It is so easy for us to say we have faith; but, believe it or not, the tests will come. Life's situations will test our faith to see whether we will put our in trust God, even though we can't see the outcome. The question that remains is "Will you pass the test?" I find that the best way to pass any test is to know God's Word and take Him at His Word . . . He never lies.

Many times I wanted to give up on my nursing endeavor, because completing the journey seemed so far off. But, my faith in God always gave me strength to press on. God placed the desire in me before I was born, and I knew He would bring it to pass.

I continued to strive toward the goal I had set for myself. After a few years of nursing school, I could finally see a light at the end of the tunnel . . . I was about to graduate from nursing school. I was beyond excitement! I was ecstatic! This was my sweet victory. I envisioned myself embarking on a new career and was looking forward to giving compassionate nursing care to my future patients. I was about to become a Licensed Practical Nurse and my hope was to pursue an RN degree two years later.

Unfortunately, my excitement was short-lived. Nothing could have prepared me for what I was about to experience . . . so I thought. Physically and emotionally I wasn't prepared, but my Heavenly Father had already prepared my spirit man (inner being) for the test that was headed my way.

≈ *1* ≈

Jesus Christ My Lord and Savior

I came into the knowledge of Jesus Christ as my Lord and Savior in 1985. As I continued my journey with Him, I began to learn more about His love, grace, and mercy for all mankind. Many times I wandered off the path of righteousness and took the wrong turn. There were times I had no clue of where I was spiritually. Some years later I found out that the Lord was breaking, making, molding, and shaping me for His purpose. I enjoyed praising and worshipping the Lord in the comfort of my home.

My life began to change. I developed a sincere love for God in my heart. I loved Him more than anything or anyone in this world. If my family, friends, and my loved ones decided they wanted nothing to do with me, it would not have mattered. I had fallen in love with my creator. I came to the conclusion that He was doing a work in me and allowing me to put Him first above everything else. I spent lots of time talking to Him, praying, and studying His word. Something began to stir up within my spirit. This feeling was strange and unexplainable. The joy, love, and peace of God was manifesting in my life. I felt the Spirit of the Lord gently moving me out of my comfort zone. He was taking me to another level in Him. I had no idea what was coming next.

Sunday Evening Service

July 7, 2002, I attended Sunday evening service at a non-denominational church called Spirit of Liberty of which I was a member. That particular service was completely different from the evening services I would usually attend. The pastor always brought forth the Word of God with clarity and understanding. That evening the congregation was asked to gather at the altar. The message of the sermon was "Tearing Down the Walls in Your Life." This message relates to the Walls of Jericho. In the Bible, God instructed Joshua to lead his army to Jericho and march around the city once a day for six days. On the seventh day, they were to march around the city seven times with the priests blowing the horns. When they would hear the long blast on the horns, the entire army was to give a mighty shout and the walls of the city would collapse (Joshua 6:3-5).

We were shouting and praising God at the altar. I was praying in my prayer language (speaking in tongues). Tears were streaming down my face as I communicated with God in the spirit. My whole being was enveloped in the spiritual realm. I had no idea what I was saying because the language was foreign to me. Only the Holy Spirit (Spirit of God) is able to give revelation of the words uttered. The communication was between me and God. Something came upon me and swung me around like a rag doll until I was slain in the spirit. This actually happened; no one touched me or laid hands on me. I had no clue of what had taken place. I went home amazed and baffled at my experience.

The next morning as I lay in bed, I realized my forearms were extremely sore. No bruising or swelling was evident. The muscles felt like they had a vigorous workout. After the initial assessment of my forearm, I pondered on the Sunday evening service. I spoke to my pastor regarding my unusual experience. He said I was at God's Throne. That statement wasn't quite clear to me. Then, all of a sudden, the Holy Spirit reminded me of God's Word, which says, "Let us then approach God's throne of grace with confidence, so that we may receive mercy and find grace to help us in our time of need" (Hebrew 4:16 NIV). It is so amazing when God's Word is manifested, because it is beyond our understanding. The human mind is unable to conceive the things of the Spirit. Personally, I believe God was preparing me for what was coming my way.

≈ 2 ≈

Unexpected Stranger

*J*uly 9, 2002, was a beautiful, bright, sunny day. It was two days following the Sunday evening service. The joy of the Lord filled my spirit as I savored the thought of reaching a long awaited threshold in my life. Ten days from this day, I would graduate from nursing school, and Oliver and I were planning a trip to Jamaica. I was joyful about all the good things that were happening in my life.

I was scheduled to report to the hospital at 2:45pm to fulfill the evening shift as part of my clinical rotation. I woke up early that morning at approximately 7 am. Due to my school schedule, I was unable to take care of certain business issues. I decided to catch up on some things that were sort of sitting on the back burner. I departed from my home at approximately

8am to run errands. Oliver had already left for work at 11pm the night before. My son, Herman, left home not long after I did. He was attending University of Louisiana at Lafayette and had a scheduled exam that day.

The area where I lived was fairly quiet and the people were friendly. Everyone knew one another within the neighborhood. Occasionally, people would stop by and ask for directions if they needed help getting to the right place. My cousins lived one lot over behind my mobile home. There was an elderly man whose home was to the left of our residence. An elderly couple lived across the highway from us. The street that ran along side of my home was a dead-end street. Therefore, traffic within the neighborhood flowed steadily with a watchful eye.

Over time, my surroundings changed. My cousins no longer lived near me. The elderly man was placed in a long-term care facility and his house was removed from the premises. The couple across the highway sold their home to a younger couple with children. I had no inkling that these changes would place me in a vulnerable position.

After completing my errands, I arrived home at approximately 11:15 am. When I entered my home, I felt an uneasy, eerie feeling, as though something evil or unsettling was present. I shrugged my shoulders as though to shake this feeling off. I then turned on some gospel music; usually this would change the disconcerted environment to a calm and peaceful atmosphere. I placed my purse, car keys, and wedding ring on the countertop. Realizing I had a little over two and a half hours left before reporting to my nursing clinical, I decided to cook a meal for Oliver and my son before leaving home.

While the meal was cooking, I began ironing my uniform in my son's bedroom. I walked back and forth from my son's room to the kitchen to check on the food I was preparing. Upon my third trip to the kitchen, there was a knock at the door. It was approximately 11:30am. I didn't check to see who was at the door before I opened it. This was a busy time of the day for me. I was rushing to get everything done before leaving home for the hospital. I had resided in this area for approximately twelve years and had no concerns about anything out of the ordinary.

When I opened the door, there was a young black man in his mid-thirties standing on the lower deck on my porch. His complexion was fair; he was neatly shaved; and it seemed like he had gotten a fresh hair cut. He was neatly dressed in denim shorts with a blue and white polo type shirt with a collar and three buttons to the upper part of the shirt. He wore sneakers with white ankle socks.

I said to the stranger standing before me, "May I help you?" His response was, "Hi, my name is Anthony. I'm from Monroe, and I'm looking for the Montgomerys. I'm supposed to do some construction work for them. Do you know where they live?" I told him I didn't know who these people were.

He then asked, "Do you think your husband might know?" I knew Oliver was at work, so immediately I said, "No, my husband has no idea who these people are." He asked if he could use my phone. I retrieved the cordless handset and gave it to him as he stood on the lower deck of the front porch. After handing the phone to him, I entered my home and closed the door behind me. He knocked on the door again and asked for the telephone directory. I handed that item to him as well. After giving this man the items he requested, I needed to check on the meal I was preparing. Therefore, I closed the glass door, which was the outer door of my mobile home.

The inner door of the mobile home was left partially opened because I didn't want to appear rude. Apparently, he must have opened the glass door because I could see him peeking through the partially opened door. He realized that I saw him peeking through the slightly opened door. He said, "I'm not going to do you anything." I didn't focus on those words at the time. My concern at the moment was to finish cooking and preparing myself in a timely fashion. I needed to get to the clinical setting on time. The rules were strict, and I did not want to be late.

I returned to the front door to retrieve the handset and telephone directory from the stranger. This man would not leave. He attempted to strike up a conversation by asking whether I had ever heard of a particular gospel choir with whom he had traveled. My immediate thought was "please leave."

Frustration began to well up within me. This man

would not go away. He even mentioned that the food I was cooking smelled good. By then, I should have realized that something wasn't quite right. He asked again, "Do you think your husband might know where the Montgomerys live?" By this time, I was irritated by his presence and his lack of understanding . . . that I had no idea who these people were or where they lived. In a frustrated tone of voice I said, "My husband is not home!"

Immediately he rushed from the lower deck of the front porch to the upper deck. This stranger was trying to force his way into my home. Suddenly, my survival instincts kicked in as I frantically applied pressure to the door using my body to close it shut! I was pushing the door from within the home as he pushed from the outside. No matter how much force I used trying to shut the door, the strength on the opposite side was far greater than mine. The struggle didn't last long. The intruder overpowered me and forced his way into my residence. What happened next was unbelievable!

≈ 3 ≈

The Attack

Once inside, he grabbed me by the throat with one hand as he pushed me against the entry door, which caused the door to slam shut. He said, "If you try anything, I have a knife, and I'll stab you in the eye." My immediate response within my spirit was, "Lord, what's going on, can't he see that I'm your child?" Everything seemed surreal! I could not believe this was happening!

He then said, "Take me to your bedroom." I knew if he took me to the bedroom, there would be no way out. My immediate response was to talk my way out of it. I said, "We don't need to go to the bedroom; we can stay right here," which was the living room area. He forced me to lie down on the living room floor with his hand still grasping my throat. He said, "Take off your panties." I said, "I can't do anything because you have your hand around my throat." He removed his hand from around my throat, and I did as I was told.

As he mentally prepared himself to sexually assault me, he whispered in my left ear, "I've been watching you." I asked, "Where did you see me?" He said, "Shut up," and I did. Apparently, his concentration was disrupted by the question. Therefore, I asked another question . . ."Can I turn the fire off from underneath the pot?" He said, "F . . . the pots." Again, I spoke to the Lord in my spirit. I said, "Lord, the house will burn down and all the evidence will be lost."

While my attacker was trying to rape me, he seemed to be having a difficult time. He appeared frustrated. I didn't attempt to fight him, because it would have resulted in a loss on my part. He was physically stronger than me. He would have gotten angry quicker and finished me off.

I thought about stabbing him with his own knife when he laid it on the floor next to me while he was trying to sexually assault me. When I picked up the knife, it had a small blade with a black handle. Instantly, I knew this weapon would only anger this man if I would have attempted to use it. He realized that I had the knife in my left hand and quickly took it from me and said "bitch." I really didn't know if he was going to take my life at this point, because I had picked up the knife. I decided to comply with his request and didn't panic.

My mind stayed on the Lord, although turmoil surrounded me. I had an unbelievable sense of peace, as if the presence of God was there. I can't really explain it. The stranger was sweating profusely, as though he was in a physical battle, even though I wasn't fighting him. He appeared to have a difficult time accomplishing his purpose for showing up at my home . . . which was to rape and kill me.

When his plan failed, he stood up while I was still lying on the living room floor. He began looking around for something. I had no idea what he was looking for. One thing I knew for sure; I was getting a good descriptive look at his face. I didn't realize he had cut a piece of the telephone cord that was connected to my son's computer. He wrapped the phone cord around my throat and tried to strangle me. As he was pulling the cord to tighten it around my throat, I grasped the cord at the front of my throat, holding on tightly with my fingers between the cord and my throat causing my attacker's plan to fail.

He decided to try something else. While I was still lying on the floor, the stranger knelt to my left side, closer to my feet, and he began removing his polo shirt. I carefully watched him as he pulled the shirt over his head, revealing a white t-shirt underneath. He said, "Stay right there, I'm not going to do you anything." I knew that was a lie from the pits of hell. But, I didn't say a word. I kept my eyes on him, watching his every move.

Once the stranger removed his polo shirt, he straddled across my shoulders, which caused my arms to be bound to my side where I could not move. I asked, "What are you doing?" Suddenly, my head involuntary turned to the right; I had just received a hard blow to the head with an object. I did not feel the blow, nor did I feel pain. I felt dazed and light headed. Again, I spoke to my Heavenly Father in my spirit. I said, "Lord, I'm your child. Please send some help."

I don't recall if I was struck in the head more than once. All I remembered was bits and pieces of the things he was doing to me. For instance, I remembered using my left leg to knock over a wicker stand which had family pictures, a vase, and other personal effects. When the wicker stand fell to the floor it startled him. He turned his head toward the falling objects. At the same time, my right leg fell to the floor from being propped on the edge of the sofa. He said, "uh-uh" (meaning no), and placed my right leg back in an upward position on the edge of the sofa. I realized this man was still trying to rape me while I was in and out of consciousness.

Before my attacker would leave me alone, he made a desperate attempt to finish me off by stomping me in my lower abdomen with his foot. Again, I did not feel pain, only pressure. Not long after I had prayed for help, my son, Herman, returned home from school. My prayer was answered!

≈ 4 ≈

Angel Sent By God

*M*y son, Herman, was 19-years-old at the time of the attack. He was attending University of Louisiana at Lafayette. On that particular day he had an exam and just happened to complete his test early. Normally, after leaving school, Herman would visit family and friends before coming home. However, he remembered what his dad said to him the night before. Oliver instructed him to return home immediately after school and begin the laundry.

The day before the attack, I spent my whole day cleaning, changing linen, doing laundry, sweeping, mopping, dusting, cooking, etc. Later that night, Herman poured himself a glass of kool-aide. He spilled a little on the floor and did not wipe up. I fussed at him for not wiping up the spill. His dad stepped in to diffuse the situation. He did as he was told and came home directly after school. Herman's purpose for coming straight home from school was far greater than doing the laundry. God's purpose was about to unfold.

When Herman arrived home from school, he parked his car in our graveled driveway. The intruder turned off the air conditioner prior to Herman's arrival in order to alert himself if someone showed up unexpectedly. When Herman got out of his car, he walked to the mailbox, which was about 10 —15 feet from the home. My attacker escaped through the rear door, which was down the hallway of the mobile home. As Herman was making his way toward the front porch of our home, he observed the gold Mitsubishi Mirage parked in our driveway. He thought the vehicle belonged to one of my friends from nursing school.

Herman entered the home and was about to reach for the handset to the cordless phone when he saw me lying on the living room floor in a pool of blood. In a horrified tone, he asked, "Mom! What's going on?" I screamed, "Herman get a knife! Get a knife! He's still in the house!"

In a raging tone of voice, Herman said, "Where is he?" He then ran out of the front door without realizing he had forgotten his car keys. Herman came back into the house to retrieve his car keys. By the time he returned to his car, my attacker had backed out of the driveway and sped off onto Highway 31, heading toward the Town of Breaux Bridge. I had great concerns about Herman chasing after this man, because I didn't want anything to happen to him. I said, "Lord, where is Herman going? Why didn't he call 911?"

Suddenly, I felt as though something or someone had lifted me off the floor and walked me to my bedroom without stumbling to call 911. I had been in and out of consciousness and didn't have the strength to do anything, much less get up from the floor on my own. God had given me the strength to walk to my bedroom to call 911. Praise His Holy Name!

The 911 Call

When I reached the bedroom, I sat on the floor with my back against the side of the bed. Amazingly, this was the place where I would always pray and spend time with God. This area was a special place for me. It was my prayer closet. Whether I needed to pray about something specific, meditate, or just bask in God's Presence . . . this is where the Lord would come and spiritually commune with me.

As I sat in my place of refuge, I reached for the phone on the bedside table to call Oliver's job. I called his job first because I needed him to know that something horrible had happened. Another reason I called his job was because I had a feeling I wouldn't be calling anyone else after the 911 call . . . and I was right.

The secretary answered the phone, I asked her to please get in touch with Oliver and have him call home. My next phone call was 911. My strength was fading, and I was experiencing shortness of breath as I made the 911 call. When the dispatcher answered my call, I explained what happened and asked for an ambulance. I don't recall the conversation between myself and the dispatcher.

The paramedics arrived and saw my condition.

They called for Air Med. I recalled one of the guys explaining to me that Air Med was on their way. When the emergency helicopter arrived, I remembered one of the paramedics pulling me by the shoulder of my dress onto the sliding board.

The next thing I remembered was the paramedic explaining to me that Air Med was going to land in my back yard, and they were going to take me out through the back door of the kitchen, and onto the emergency vehicle. I found out sometime later that the paramedics said I would not survive due to a significant amount of blood loss.

The moment I arrived at Lafayette General Medical Center the emergency crew came out to get me and immediately took me to the emergency room. I don't recall who the emergency personnel were, but I do remember Dr. Terry A. Cromwell and Dr. Thomas V. Bertuccini. They were the surgeons caring for me. I overheard bits and pieces of the conversations going on around me. Both of my eyes were swollen shut by that time.

One of the doctors mentioned that I had a hematoma (blood clot) to the forehead area. I then heard him say he would try and aspirate it with a syringe. He was able to remove 5cc of blood from the affected area. For some reason or another he had a concern about trying to extract more blood from my forehead. I recall the doctors saying I also had a laceration which was 6cm deep to the left frontal area of my head. They also said the x-ray showed a hairline fracture to the frontal area of my skull.

The doctors discussed among themselves what procedures they would use to treat my condition. Then I heard the two physicians talk about taking me into surgery for debridement (cleaning out dead, damaged, or infected tissues) to the wound on my forehead and suturing it. That was the plan at hand, and it was followed through and completed successfully.

≈ 5 ≈

The Healing Process

O nce the procedure was completed, I was admitted to the Oncology Unit due to an overflow on the Neurology Unit. A good friend of mine, Patricia C., was my admitting nurse on the Oncology Unit. She took very good care of me, as well as the other medical team.

I spoke with her sometime later after the attack. As she began to describe my appearance upon arrival to the Oncology Unit, she broke down in tears and said, "My cousin, you were covered in blood from your head to your feet." As she continued to sob, I felt her amazing compassion as she gave an account of the horrendous sight of my outer shell, as I lay on the stretcher before her.

One thing she didn't know was that my spirit man was still intact. I couldn't help but think of Jesus . . . how He was whipped and crucified for us. Jesus was bloody from the crown of His head to the sole of His feet as He carried His cross to Cavalry.

This is how I saw myself . . . in the image of Jesus' suffering. I didn't see the circumstance as she spoke; I saw the glory of God all over the circumstance. The situation looked bad through the eyes of man, but God was about to perform a miracle. His awesome glory was about to be revealed. He was about to take a situation that looked hopeless and turn it around.

As a nursing student, I knew all too well about the medical complications that could have occurred. I was at risk for infection, swelling of the brain, hematoma (blood clot), aneurysm (rupture of a weakened blood vessel), permanent brain damage, a stroke, even death.

Thanks to Almighty God! The Bible says, "The spirit of a man will sustain him in sickness; but, who can bear a broken spirit?" (Proverbs 18:14 NKJ)

The following day I was transferred from Oncology

to the Neurology Unit. The nurse settled me into my room. My eyes were still swollen shut. I was unable to see the damage caused to my face. Perhaps God wanted it that way. It was at that point that I let go and rested in the Lord.

Sometime later, my stepdaughter, Olivia, told me that my face was severely swollen. I also recall my sister, Dorothy, telling me that my face looked like the elephant man. In speaking to my daughter, Tamika, regarding my hospital stay, she said that when she walked into my hospital room I was unrecognizable. She added that my head was swollen; my eyes were black and blue and swollen shut; and my appearance was that of an alien. Oliver said the swelling to my forehead began decreasing after my mom applied a warm towel dipped in a mixture of Epsom Salt and water. Thank God for home remedies and a loving, caring mother. Although my body had gone through a physical battle, my spirit remained strong. I kept my faith and hope in God. He's the only anchor I know.

My family members were in the hallway waiting to visit me. The nurse asked if I wanted them to come in. I asked her to allow them to come in two at a time. As each family member entered the room, I recognized their voices and communicated with them until the last one visited me.

It occurred to me that the visitation with my family seemed like a visitation at a funeral. Each of them stood at the foot of my bed to view my current condition. I could discern the sympathy in their voices. The words spoken were few, as though they were dismayed and at a loss for words. I felt the compassion that radiated from every word spoken. Peace filled the atmosphere as my loved ones tried to console me.

I couldn't help but wonder what they were viewing with their natural eyes as they visited me. I must admit, they handled it well. I was curious about my facial appearance, but I was unable to view it for myself because I couldn't see. As my family visited me, I politely asked them if my face looked bad. A few of them found it better to change the subject, while others avoided answering the question. Perhaps I would have done the same thing if I was in their position.

Nevertheless, I was blessed by their presence. I am

truly grateful to everyone who took the time to visit me and especially grateful to those who prayed for me.

I was not left alone during my hospital stay. A family member stayed with me at all times. I was also listed under an assumed name, due to the fact that my attacker was still at large.

I don't recall everyone who stayed with me while being in the hospital. One night in particular, I remember waking up in the middle of the night to Oliver crying at my bedside. His right forearm was on the bedrail while his forehead rested upon his arm. I could hear him weeping. I asked "Why are you crying?" I don't recall his response. I said "Don't cry, everything will be okay." After saying these words, I immediately went back to sleep.

On the sixth day of my hospital stay, the nurse came into my room and said I was being discharged because the doctor said I was ready to go home. My family began bickering with one another about who I was going home with. I began to cry. My injuries weren't as painful as watching my family bicker with one another. I remembered what it was like to rest peacefully in the Lord. In His rest there is complete peace and tranquility—no worries about anything.

While recuperating from my injuries, The Lord spoke to my spirit and said, "Give no thought to food, drink, or clothing." (Matthew 6:25). He was mainly telling me to rest in His arms and not to worry about everyday life. After hearing these words, I totally surrendered and allowed the Lord to have His way in my life. It was awesome! I imagine this to be similar to that of toddlers when they trust their parents to safely carry them in their arms. I felt safe and secure in Jesus' arms.

The following day, after my release from the hospital, I was asked to go down to the Sheriff's Department to give a description of my attacker and an account of what happened during the attack. One of the detectives drew a computer composite based on my description. I also explained what happened during the attack. The detectives took pictures of the bruises on my face and neck caused by my attacker. Once Oliver and I left the police station, we returned to my sister-in-law's home where we were currently staying.

I remained in the spiritual realm for quite some time. The pain in my head was excruciating, and I couldn't tolerate noise.

I rested fairly well during the daytime. But, my nights were horrible. I was restless and was unable to sleep due to head pain. The nights were so long it seemed like daylight would never come. There was absolutely no comfortable resting position for my head. I tried sleeping on several different pillows while lying in bed, but to no avail. Then I tried sleeping in a recliner, which didn't help either.

Next, I decided to sleep on the floor. I ended up right back in the bed. This episode was so awful. I wouldn't wish this on my worst enemy. I could only imagine what I was putting my family through. They went beyond measure to help me in every possible way. My children constantly checked up on me, and Oliver was patient with me. No matter what I went through, he hung in there. I thank God for all of them.

Family and friends called and wanted to come over to visit with me while I was staying at my sister-in-laws home. I was in no condition to visit with anyone. I was unable to engage in lengthy conversations. It was difficult for me to receive and process information due to the head trauma. Too much talking was overwhelming for me and caused my head to hurt.

I understood my family and friends' sympathy and compassion towards me, as well as their wanting to be there to comfort me during the most difficult time in my life. I'd like to take this time to apologize from the deepest part of my heart, and let my family, friends, and associates know that their thoughts, prayers, gifts, and presence were sincerely appreciated and uplifting.

No one except God knew what I was experiencing. He was the only one I could depend on to heal me from all my infirmities.

As we tried to pick up the pieces of our lives, it was evident that we were not going back to our home. Oliver gathered family and friends to help pack up all of our belongings, and placed them in storage. The mobile home and property were sold. We continued to live with family members until we got an apartment six months later.

As much as I wanted to complain about the dramatic changes that affected my life, I continued to keep a positive attitude. I often thought about the women with whom I shared this experience. All of them were doing positive things in their lives. I took the time to look at the fact that they have gone on to be with the Lord and didn't have to suffer from the wounds and scars they endured.

On the other hand, there were times I felt left behind. I literally suffered with pain and agony from this head trauma. I frequently experienced episodes of vertigo. These dizzy spells became a part of my everyday life. My speech became slurred. At times when I spoke, my words were out of order or backwards.

I began seeking professional help to relieve my symptoms. I went to see a physician at the New Orleans Charity Hospital. Lo and behold, the doctor I saw also had vertigo from a motorcycle accident!

Immediately, I directed my focus on God. I said, "Okay God . . . this is no accident that this man happened to be my doctor on this given date and time. What are you trying to tell me?"

The Lord was trying to show me this man's situation. He had vertigo and continued to work in his profession. He did not let his situation hinder him from doing what God called him to do . . . take care of the sick. This man did not give up because of his circumstance. I received the lesson at hand.

God had placed the desire within me to become a nurse when I was just a child. It was my passion to work in that profession. God's love dwelled within me, and I wanted to share that light of hope with my future patients. I decided not to let my current circumstance stop me from working as a nurse. There's a purpose for everything that happens in life, and I knew God's purpose would be fulfilled. It was.

I began working as a nurse with the skills from nursing school and talent from God. The most rewarding part of my job was encouraging and praying with and for my patients as I cared for them. As I pressed my way toward God's purpose for my life, He healed me from the dizzy spells. Praise God! I cannot tell you the exact date or time it went away. I just realized one day that it wasn't there anymore.

≈ 6 ≈

The Transition

 This period was a tough time for me and my family. We were constantly moving from one family member's home to another. These times affected us emotionally, physically, and spiritually. Prior to getting an apartment, we were living with one of my sisters in Youngsville, Louisiana.

I recall not wanting to have a conversation with anyone. I only wanted to communicate with God because there were questions I needed answered. I remained in the bedroom where I slept and waited for the Holy Spirit. I felt such a desperate need for him to come and talk with me.

While I was waiting for an encounter with the Holy Spirit, my thoughts remained on God as I reflected on the attack. Deep within my being, I knew that the Spirit of the living God was present as the attack was taking place. The whole experience of the attack seemed like a re-enactment on a television program.

America's Most Wanted was one of the shows Oliver and I often watched. During my attack, the re-enactments of that particular show came to mind. I wasn't afraid. My spirit was at peace, and I was in constant communication with the Holy Spirit. The Bible says, "You will keep *him* in perfect peace, *whose* mind is stayed on You, because he trusts in You" (Isaiah 26:3 NKJV). It's amazing to actually experience the truth of God's Word. His Word is real . . . I can testify to that!

Finally, the Holy Spirit showed up, and we communicated. I began asking him questions. I asked, "Lord what happened?" He responded with His Word saying, "Have you considered my servant Job?" In the Bible Job was considered a righteous man of God. He suffered many things. But, no matter what Job went through he did not turn his back on God; he remained faithful. Then God blessed Job with a double portion of everything the devil had taken from him. When the

Holy Spirit said, "Have you considered my servant Job?" immediately I knew that it was a test of my faith. Like Job, I stayed with God and did not waver. In fact, I drew closer to Him. He was a safe haven for me.

I realized God had been a safe haven for me long before the attack. In the early years of my Christian walk, when all seemed well, I wanted to live the way I once did; which was doing my own thing apart from God. But, when trouble came, I would run back to God.

One day I made up my mind that staying with Him was the safest place to be. My relationship with Him had become personal. I enjoyed my time with Him and the people He placed in my path. I took time everyday to come away from the busy moments of life just to communicate with Him. My communication with the Lord did not cease after the attack; it grew stronger.

My next question was, "Who was he?" The Lord said "the enemy." I understood the words to a certain degree, because I knew the enemy was Satan. The curiosity of my flesh wanted specifics. I needed specific details of who did this to me and why. I didn't get the answer for which I was looking, because God operates on His timing. I believed at some point the answers to my questions would come later.

I often became upset and cried; I didn't understand why this man interrupted my life. I was about to graduate from nursing school in two weeks and was looking forward to working in my profession. My family was anxiously anticipating my graduation day, and so was I.

One thing I knew for sure; God knows me better than I know myself. Day by day He began revealing things to me, and it was always based on His Word. I didn't always have my bible at hand, but His Word was stored in my heart.

God ministered to me by saying, "If you cling to your life, you will lose it, and if you let your life go, you will save it" (Luke 17:33 NIV). I wasn't clear on how this statement applied to my situation. The only thing I figured out from that scripture was that, during the attack, I did not fight off my assailant. Instead, I surrendered my life into God's hands. I knew I would lose the battle if I tried to fight him; he was stronger than me. I prayed, as I mentally prepared myself to exit from this world into the spirit world—if that was God's will.

My main concern was my family finding me dead and not knowing what happened, or who killed me. Other than that, if God was ready for me, I was ready to go. I just wanted my family to be okay and accept God's will for my life. After all, I am His creation, and I am His child, as well as His beloved. All of the other women were God's beloved as well.

≈ 7 ≈

My Attacker Revealed

The afternoon of May 2003, Detective Arthur Boyd, Detective Marcus Guidry, and Lieutenant Rena Williams arrived at my residence. As they sat on the living room couch across from Oliver and me, Detective Boyd began to share new information received from the crime lab. He said the DNA marker found on the collar of my dress, matched the DNA found on the other women who had been murdered.

I was in a state of shock! Nothing could have prepared me for this moment. On one hand, I was pleased that the pieces of the puzzles were finally coming together. On the other hand, the reality of this whole scenario was more than I could handle. Baffled and speechless, I broke down into tears.

From this point on, everything that was said went over my head. I was in another world. In my mind, I wondered if my attacker knew I was still alive . . . and if so, would he come looking for me. I began to panic as different thoughts went through my head. This man had all of my personal information. He stole my purse from my home the day of the attack.

As Rena tried to console me, one of the detectives mentioned that the Baton Rouge Task Force wanted to speak with me. I was distraught, confused, and definitely lacking trust in most people. I wanted to hide in a place where no one could find me. I definitely did not want to meet with the task force or anyone else for that matter. I did not want my identity out in the public, because I was concerned my attacker would use the information he had in his possession to seek me out.

I told the detective that I couldn't meet with the task force just yet. He said that if I didn't speak with the task force voluntarily, they were going to subpoena me. Reluctantly, I did agree to meet them later that week. My only request was to speak with a female, which was honored.

A profile analyst by the name of Mary Ellen O' Toole met with me at the Holiday Inn Express in Henderson, Louisiana. A male was also present at that meeting. However, I don't recall who he was. Ms. O'Toole introduced herself to me and began asking me a series of questions. She asked me to explain to her exactly what happened and describe the demeanor of my attacker before and after he entered my home.

I explained to Ms O'Toole everything that had taken place from beginning to end. She asked me the same questions over and over. As I continued to answer her questions, the scene of the attack began to replay over and over in my mind. Ms O'Toole was trying to put together the behavioral profile of my attacker.

After all of the draining questions, a sketch artist by the name of Debbie Brasseaux was called in to draw a receding hairline, which was lacking on the computer composite of my attacker. That sketch was given to Law Enforcement. Once that was done, my meeting with the profile analyst was over.

The next day, Detective Arthur Boyd contacted me

with regard to a press conference, which was going to air concerning the information I had given the profile analyst. He gave me his word that he would notify me in advance before the press conference aired. I know he did his best to keep his word, but unfortunately, I was told about the press conference ten minutes before it aired. It wasn't Detective Boyd's fault regarding the short notice of the televised press conference. He also found out about it shortly before it was televised.

I was beside myself, and I was not mentally prepared for the information that was about to go forth. While watching the broadcast, I kept saying . . . . .please don't say my name; please, please, don't say my name! Suddenly, my name was mentioned. I became frantic! I said, "Now, everybody knows my name, and that I'm a surviving victim of The Southwest Louisiana Serial Killer. I was hoping they would find him before exposing who I was. Most everyone from my hometown knew that I was attacked in my home. But on a larger scale, many people did not know of my attack or who I was. I did not want to be pushed out into the media frenzy.

Many different thoughts went through my head.

By then, I figured my attacker probably knew I was alive. I wondered if he was angry because his plan to murder me had failed. I also wondered whether he would come back and finish me off. I really did not feel safe, so I called Rena, my victim's advocate. I explained to her that I had been feeling uneasy since the information regarding the Southwest Louisiana Serial Killer was released to the public. She phoned Detective Boyd and told him about my concerns. Detective Boyd called me after discussing the matter with his supervisor. I was offered to go to my son's residence in Kentucky until my attacker was caught.

My victim's advocate picked me up from my apartment and drove me to the airport in New Orleans where I boarded the plane for Kentucky. My son, Djuanas, picked me up from the airport upon my arrival. I stayed with him and his family for a few days.

The second day after my arrival in Kentucky, I received a phone call at approximately 3:00 am from Detective Boyd. He said he was emailing a line-up of six men and asked if I could look at the photos carefully to see if I recognized any of the faces. As I lay in bed, I prayed and asked God to please let me be able to pick my attacker out of the line-up because it was approaching one year since my attack. I definitely did not want to accuse the wrong man.

I received the email about fifteen or twenty minutes later. Carefully and diligently, I looked at each photo before moving on to the next picture. I observed the hairline, eyes, nose, ears, facial structure, shade of complexion, hair color, and also the mustache.

I remembered specific features about him, such as the shape of his nose as he faced forward and sideways. He had a fresh haircut with well trimmed edges. I recalled the shape of his lips and the thin mustache. I studied his face during my attack to seal his appearance in my memory.

He stood outside the door of my mobile home on that bright, sunny day where his features were extremely clear from his head to his feet. In addition, my eyelids remained closed for days after the blow to the head, and I continuously saw mental images of his face. That's how I was able to pick him out of the line-up. I thank God for bringing everything back to my remembrance and answering my prayer.

After carefully examining all six faces in the lineup, number five matched my attacker perfectly. My son got Detective Boyd on the phone, and I spoke with him. I explained to him that my attacker was number five in the line-up. He asked whether I was sure and did I need more time to look at the line-up. I said, "Without a shadow of doubt, number five was the man who attacked me."

I asked him if there was a name to go with that face. Detective Boyd said his name was Derrick Todd Lee. I was happy to know that the pieces of this puzzle were finally coming together. Derrick Todd Lee's picture in the line-up was exactly the same as the day he stood on my front porch. I did not have any problems identifying him. I felt a sigh of relief to know that my attacker was identified, which would probably lead to his capture and arrest.

Djuanas printed the line-up from their computer, and I circled the number five above the picture. Then, I returned to bed with little interest in falling asleep. I began thanking God for His awesomeness and for assigning my case to Detective Boyd. I'm grateful he answered the call and worked diligently on my case.

The next day Djuanas sent the information to Detective Boyd. I petitioned the Heavenly Father again. This time I prayed and asked, "God, please do not let a year go by from the day that I was attacked before this man is caught," and again my prayer was answered.

≈ 8 ≈

The Arrest

*D*errick Todd Lee was captured in Atlanta, Georgia, on Tuesday May 27, 2003. He was apprehended at 8:45 pm at a tire shop. According to the media he did not resist the arresting officer. He was taken to jail in Fulton County where he stayed overnight.

When I heard of his capture, there were no words to describe how I felt. I shouted with joy and kept praising God. For the first time since my attack, I felt like a load had been lifted. Derrick Todd Lee was off the streets.

Although I was confident about returning home, my journey down this long road was just beginning. My son, Herman, and I would have to testify when the trial began.

The following week Derrick Todd Lee was extradited back to Louisiana to face charges for the attack on my life. Mixed emotions welled up within me. The reality of seeing this man since my attack made me nervous. At the same time, I was angry, because he disrupted my life. I didn't understand *why* he did this to me and the other women. This man attacked us in a violent and vicious manner—for no apparent reason, except for his mental derangement.

Oliver and I received a call asking us to come to the St. Martin Parish Assistant District Attorney's office to view the visual recording of the interrogation of Derrick Todd Lee, which took place in Atlanta. He had gained weight since the day I saw him on my front porch that warm summer of July 2002.

I was hoping that during the interrogation Lee would provide answers to my question . . . *why?* I listened intently as I anxiously waited for him to tell the truth about my attack.

He spoke about dating many women such as white

women, and women of high social status. He even said he was dating one of the women he murdered.

I found this to be an insult to that victim's family. This was a lie according to the victim's family. Derrick Todd Lee spoke about a woman he dated who was embarrassed to be seen with him in public. He continued to rant about women who crushed his ego.

I don't recall the name of the detective who interrogated Derrick Todd Lee. During questioning, the detective asked, "Derrick, everybody has a story to tell, what's your story?" Derrick Todd Lee said, "I got no story to tell." He made a gesture with his hand as though he was closing a book and said, "The book is closed."

The profile analyst, Mary Ellen O'Toole, who interviewed me, also questioned Derrick Todd Lee. I don't recall the questions that were asked, but this lustful demonic spirit that engulfed this man was literally flirting with this woman in the interrogating room. I shivered with fright as I watched Derrick Todd Lee's demeanor change from macho, when speaking to the male interrogator, to flirting with the female profile analyst. All of this was being recorded, and he didn't even care. It was evident to see the evil tactics of this man and how he was calculating. He was asked questions regarding the murders.

Lee denied having anything to do with the crimes of which he was accused. He even denied having anything to do with the attack on my life. Unfortunately, the answer to my question "why" was never revealed.

≈ 9 ≈

The Trial and Conviction

The trial date slowly drew near. The first trial was scheduled August 5, 2004, in West Baton Rouge Parish, in the town of Port Allen, Louisiana. Derrick Todd Lee was going on trial for the murder of Geralyn DeSota. I had been subpoenaed to testify against him.

I began to feel anxious, knowing the task that lay before me was a difficult one. Although I knew the Lord was with me, I still felt apprehensive on my journey. I really did not know what to do. Oliver and I did not communicate much about the trial, or the whole ordeal for that matter. He didn't like revisiting that gruesome day. I prayed to God for guidance.

One Sunday morning after church service at

Destiny of Faith Christian Center, I went to my pastor and asked whether I could schedule an appointment to meet with him and his wife. I was a new member at the church, and no one really knew me or my situation. He advised me to call the church office to schedule an appointment. I called the office the next day and was given an appointment to come in a couple of days later.

The pastor's wife and I met in a conference room at the church. I explained to her what had happened to me on July 9, 2002. I mentioned that I needed lots of prayers as I was soon to go through the trial process. I told her this was a difficult journey for me, and I could not do it alone.

The pastor's wife understood, and she assigned her mother-in law, who is a mighty intercessor, to assist me. This woman was truly a prayer warrior on my behalf. Her prayers were fervent. God's word says that the effectual, fervent prayer of a righteous man availeth much (James 5:15). I believe this with all my being. I spoke with the pastor's mother at the next Sunday Service. She gave me her phone number and asked me to call her.

Prior to Derrick Todd Lee's capture, I continually prayed, asking God to allow me to see my attacker face to face in the courtroom. I needed him to see my face and recall what he had done to me. I wanted to look him in the eye! I hoped the day of my attack replayed in his mind as he realized I was a witness to who he really was and what he had done. I thank God for His Amazing Grace . . . for without Him, I don't know how I would have made it.

The day before the trial I cried practically all day, because I didn't think I was quite ready to face all these people in the courtroom. When I finally took a break from crying, I picked up the phone and called my pastor's mom. When she answered the phone, I reminded her of who I was. She asked how I was doing, and I said, "Not so well." I told her I had been crying all morning. She wanted to know what was troubling me.

I said, "Tomorrow I am scheduled to go to trial and testify. I have to tell this humiliating story to strangers." She then asked, "What specifically would you like me to do for you?" I said, "If you cannot physically come with me to trial, please stand in the gap and pray on my behalf as I go through the trial process. She agreed and then began praying with me. Once I hung up the phone, I felt a sense of peace, and I knew in my spirit that everything would be okay.

The next morning my family and I left Lafayette, Louisiana, to meet Chester Cedar and police escorts in Henderson, Louisiana. I was totally numb to everything going on around me. All I knew was that God had given me this specific assignment for His divine purpose.

When we arrived at the courthouse, we parked in a designated area. My family and I, the St. Martin Parish Assistant District Attorney, and my victim's advocate began walking toward the courthouse. Reporters from different TV stations had their cameras rolling. I still could not fathom the idea of the direction my life was taking.

As I walked up onto the courthouse steps, I was met and embraced by the family of Charlotte Murray Pace and Pam Kinamore. The embrace was warm and welcoming. I sensed their heartache when they spoke. They continued thanking me for the strength and courage I had shown for coming forward to testify. Little did they know that it was Jesus Christ magnifying Himself through me. Had I relied on my own strength and courage, many people would have been disappointed. I would not have made it. I would have fallen apart under all the pressure that was coming my way. The whole ordeal would have been too much for me to handle without God in my life.

Once we entered the courtroom, we were taken to a floor on the upper level inside the courthouse where Herman and I waited until it was time to testify. I don't recall the length of time we waited before we were called into the court room.

He and I went in to testify one at a time. It seemed like the wait lasted forever. My mind was focused on the task ahead. When it was time for me to testify, I began to feel butterflies in the pit of my stomach. But, this didn't stop me from going forth to tell the truth.

I was sworn in before the questioning began. Then I sat in the witness chair facing everyone in the courtroom. I was a little nervous; all these people were watching me! Chester Cedar was the first to question me. He took me back to the date of my attack (July 9, 2002). He asked me to explain what happened on that day. I explained what happened. After the questioning was over by Mr. Cedars, the defense attorney for Derrick Todd Lee stood up from where he was sitting. He began walking towards me.

As he made his way to the witness stand to question me, I grew angry within my spirit. I thought to myself, "How could he have the nerve to ask me anything when this man killed all these women and tried to kill me?" I got a hold of myself and began praying. I said, "God, you know I'm upset right now. Please remove the anger and help me to answer the questions," and He did.

The defense attorney asked me many questions. Among them there was one particular question I will never forget. He asked, "Didn't you say Derrick Todd Lee was wearing socks up to the calf of his leg?" I said, "No, he was wearing ankle socks." He continued to try and twist my words. Out of frustration, I asked him if it was more important to remember his socks rather than his face! I don't recall what his response was, but I'm sure he felt like a heel.

While he was still questioning me, the prosecution and defense attorneys had to approach the judge's bench. As the attorneys were talking to the judge, I stared at Derrick Todd Lee with anger in my eyes while saying to myself, "Look at the mess you've created!"

This man was nonchalant. He did not express remorse for what he had done. Although he had not been convicted at the time, I believed in my heart that he had committed these murders.

There are many reasons why I believed that Derrick Todd Lee committed these murders. I will give you three reasons that will support my belief:

The first reason was that Derrick Todd Lee cut a telephone cord at my place of residence and tried to strangle me with it, but he did not succeed. He took the piece of telephone cord with him when he fled from my home. That same piece of telephone cord was found in the area where Pam Kinamore's body was discovered. Evidence proved that it was the piece of telephone cord from my home. The remaining telephone cord from my residence was placed into evidence. When detectives matched it to the piece that was found near Pam Kinamore's body, it fit perfectly.

The second reason was that Charlotte Murray Pace was stabbed 81 times, including the eye area. During my attack, Derrick Todd Lee pulled out a small paring knife with a black handle from his back pocket. He threatened to stab me in the eye if I attempted to do anything foolish.

The third reason was that Geralyn Desoto was stomped in her abdomen with his bloody boot. His boot print was left on her clothing. I was also stomped in my lower abdomen, which caused internal bleeding to that area. More evidence was revealed during the trial, which most people knew nothing about.

Once I finished testifying, I was removed from the courtroom. Now it was Herman's turn to take the witness stand. He witnessed the car parked in our driveway driven by Derrick Todd Lee on that fateful day. Herman's testimony was based on his description of the vehicle, which was a Gold Mitsubishi Mirage. He said the front grill was damaged. He mentioned that a white piece of telephone cord was dangling out of a partially lowered back window behind the driver's seat.

When Herman entered our home he did not see my attacker, because Lee ran out the back door, got into his car, and fled the scene. Herman's testimony was crucial to identifying the vehicle involved in this crime. I'm proud of him for observing the necessary details of the car which helped to get Derrick Todd Lee off the streets.

I also testified at the trial of Charlotte Murray Pace. This trial took place in East Baton Rouge Parish. My experience in that trial was similar to that of Geralyn DeSoto. The District Attorney said I would only be able to testify in the trials, but would not be able to sit in the courtroom to hear the testimonies, because it would conflict with other information I needed to present. Although I was curious about the evidence presented during the trial, I accepted their advice and waited for the outcome. Derrick Todd Lee was convicted of second degree murder for the death of Geralyn DeSoto in West Baton Rouge Parish and capital murder for the death of Charlotte Murray Pace in East Baton Rouge Parish.

I thought of the other women everyday, because I shared this horrific ordeal along with them. No matter how exasperating going to trial became, I began to see it from a different perspective . . . as something positive. I began to see it as a mission for justice, not only for myself, but for my family, the other women, and their families as well. I depended on God more than I ever had before. From that day on, every step I took, I did it with God's purpose in mind—JUSTICE.

≈ *10* ≈

The Sentencing

Now it was the judge's moment to hand down the sentencing for Derrick Todd Lee's conviction. Lee had already been sentenced to mandatory life imprisonment for the murder of Geralyn Desoto. For the murder of Charlotte Murray Pace, he was given the death penalty. I wish I would have been present when the judge rendered his decision. I could only imagine the relief of the victim's families to know that he would never be able to harm another woman.

Once the trial for Charlotte Murray Pace was over, and the death sentence was rendered, the devil taunted me for three days. The enemy said, "You call yourself a Christian. Now this man will be put to death." The enemy was trying to make me feel guilty because

Derrick Todd Lee was sentenced to life in prison and given the death penalty.

I struggled with those thoughts for three days as I considered *who I was*. I love the Lord with my whole heart, and I was a nurse who believed in life. I actually felt guilty that he had a death sentence as though it was my fault. I communicated with the Lord concerning the matter.

Finally, the Lord gave me peace about it, and I spoke back to the enemy. I said, "Devil, all I did was tell the truth. Derrick Todd Lee sealed his own fate." From that day on, the enemy did not trouble me about it anymore. The scripture in James 4:7 says, "Submit yourself therefore unto God, resist the devil, and he will flee from you" . . . and he did.

I also had an overwhelming desire to address Derrick Todd Lee about what he had done to me; but, I never had the chance. If I had been able to do so, I would have asked him what possessed him to knock on my door that day. "Why?" was the biggest question on my mind. Why would he invade the lives of women he knew nothing about? What did he have to gain from interrupting my life and the lives of innocent women? What was his motive for the attack on the women when he himself has a mother, a sister, and a wife? How did he face his mom, as a female, knowing in his heart what he did to destroy the lives of other females?

I often wondered how he would feel if someone attacked his mom or any of the females in his life? Even though I knew I may never have the answers to my questions, I prayed this simple prayer; while he was still on his killing spree. My prayer was, "Lord, whenever Derrick Todd Lee puts his hands around the throat of another woman, let him see his mother's face and then make a decision whether or not he will go forth with his intentions." I can't say whether or not the prayer was answered. Only Derrick Todd Lee would know the answer to that question.

≈ *11* ≈

Derrick Todd Lee

(The Evil That Lurked Within)

An evil force found its way from St Francisville, La., to Baton Rouge, La., and across the Atchafalaya Basin to the small towns of Breaux Bridge, La., and Grand Coteau, La. Along its dark and conniving journey, stretching across Interstate 10, many lives were senselessly claimed. Who could have imagined that this unpredictable entity would bring destruction to so many families . . . unknown to one another?

This demon spirit masked itself as an ordinary human being with an innocent appearance. It spoke calmly, dressed neatly, and its appearance was unremarkable . . . nothing to suggest anything out of the ordinary. In my case, he was a person claiming to be lost.

As I look back over my encounter with Derrick Todd Lee, I realize he was not physically lost but was spiritually lost. Somewhere along his life's journey, he allowed the devil to control his mind, body, and soul. His disruptive behavior from the past revealed demonic training in action.

According to *www.trutv.com*, Lee was no stranger to law enforcement. His arrest and related incidents go as far back as 1992—2000. In November 1992, he was arrested for illegal entry and burglary of a Zachary residence. In January 1993, he was arrested for breaking into the home of a seventy-year-old man whom he beat with a stick and robbed. In July 1993, Lee was sentenced to one year in prison for burglary. In September 1995, he was arrested for a peeping incident and resisting arrest. During the same month, Lee was arrested for stealing from a Salvation Army Thrift Store. In December 1999, he received a suspended sentence on a misdemeanor stalking charge. In January 2000, he was accused of attempted first-degree murder after severely kicking and stomping his girlfriend, Cassandra Green, at a bar after an argument over Lee's advances toward another woman.

His unruly behavior escalated into a whirlwind that took him to another level. Instead of the petty crimes that led him in and out of jail like a revolving door, he decided to become a roaring loin seeking whom he may devour . . . just like SATAN. He had no inclination that the devil was using him just to set him up. In the end, he had to pay for the murderous crimes he committed.

The women who lost their lives by the hands of Derrick Lee, along with me as a victim, did absolutely nothing to him to deserve such a cruel and violent attack upon our lives. Our families were deeply wounded by Derrick Todd Lee's actions. But, what did he gain? He also wounded his own family in the process.

I heard a minister preach that God gives us free will. The minister took it a step further and said, "If we take a closer look at the words 'free will', the only free will we have is to serve God or Satan. If we choose to do whatever we want, we are still serving

Satan. When we serve God, we choose His will over ours.

Derrick Todd Lee chose to do whatever he wanted . . . . steal, kill, and destroy. This is the devil's plan for all mankind. I praise God, because He is still on the throne and is in control. What the devil meant for bad, God turned it around for good . . . for me, my family, and the families of the other women who have gone to be with the Lord.

JUSTICE PREVAILED! Within unpleasant situations there is always a lesson to learn.

I can't speak for anyone else, but I have learned many lessons from this horrifying event. For one, I've learned to live each day with a purpose and enjoy every minute of it. As strange as it may seem, I am consciously aware of every detail of my day, because I am constantly waiting, listening, and watching for a movement of God. He moves in mysterious ways . . . ways unimaginable to us.

When the next day shows up, if God wills it, I purpose myself to enjoy it as though it is my last day on earth and let go of the day gone by. I refuse to let anyone rob me of the abundant life in Christ Jesus that God has promised me . . . especially Derrick Todd Lee.

I've also learned how to forgive. I sincerely, whole-heartedly forgive this man for what he has done to me. The Lord taught me an important lesson about forgiveness. I knew I had to forgive this man whose mission was to rape and kill me. The Bible clearly says that if we don't forgive others, God will not forgive us for our wrongs. Therefore, I said, "Lord, I forgive Derrick Todd Lee. For I know, Lord, that if I don't forgive him, you will not forgive me." The Lord's response was, "Do you SINCERELY forgive him?" The word "sincerely" caused me to pause. I searched my heart and found out I really wanted to forgive him. However, I was concerned about the memories of the brutal attack revisiting me and whether or not I could get past that barrier. But, I didn't want to be plagued with resentment.

As I meditated on forgiveness, I discovered the truth within myself. I realized that as I would think about what happened to me and how Derrick Todd

Lee had interrupted my life, I would continue to feel anger. That was an awesome revelation for me. It showed me that there was a deeper level of forgiveness that I needed to release toward him. Now I knew what I needed to do. I went down on my knees, and I asked God to help me to forgive Derrick Todd Lee with a sincere heart . . . and He did.

I now harbor no anger or resentment toward Derrick Todd Lee. I feel sad for him. The destruction he caused in the life of others ultimately found its way back to him. My arms were bound to my side as he straddled across my chest to deliver the first blow to my head. Now he is bound behind prison walls, staring at the iron bars before him with no one to call on but the Lord Jesus . . . just like I did, and I pray that he does.

There's hope for him and salvation for his soul. God hates sin, but loves the sinner. God is LOVE. He forgives every kind of sin if we repent. The only sin He will not forgive is blasphemy of the Holy Spirit. In other words, He does not forgive one who disrespects or ridicules the Holy Spirit. He says, for whoever calls upon the name of The Lord shall be saved (Romans

10:13). That's God's promise, not mine. His word is alive and very active in the earth.

The family of Derrick Todd Lee was present at the trials. Many questions stirred up within me. I couldn't begin to imagine what was going through the mind of Lee's mother. I wondered whether she thought her son was falsely accused. No parent wants to believe the worst of their children. In fact, sometimes we refuse to see the truth regarding our children's actions.

Oliver said he heard one of Lee's family members say, "She's lying" . . . referring to me as I was testifying. Oliver mentioned to me that the remark angered him, and he responded with an unpleasant comment. I'm happy he contained himself during the court proceedings; otherwise, he would have been removed from the courtroom.

The pain and anger of the victims' families filled the atmosphere of the courtroom. Comments were made from different family members. One of the family members said, "Derrick Todd Lee should be grateful that law enforcement got to him first." Another one said, "All I need is five minutes with him." When I testified that Lee's attempt to rape me was unsuccessful because he could not achieve an erection, a man in the courtroom found it amusing. He laughed and added a comment. The judge summoned him out of the courtroom.

It was difficult for me, my family, and the families of the other women to contain our emotions and verbal expressions without getting reprimanded by the judge presiding over the case. As difficult as it was, only the Lord knew what our thoughts were and how our hearts screamed for revenge. I'm sure that didn't please God. Nothing could have eased the pain and anguish that scarred the hearts of these families left to grieve for their loved ones.

I wondered if closure would ever come to all of us affected by this tragedy. I recall Assistant District Attorney Chester Cedars saying to me that families never truly get closure for the brutal death of a loved one. I've come to realize that the only closure I know is the peace of mind that comes with knowing that The Southwest Louisiana Serial Killer, Derrick Todd Lee would be caught, convicted, and sentenced . . . ending his killing spree.

As for the rest of us affected by the evil whirlwind that swept through our lives, we must press forward, remembering the innocent victims that were taken away from the ones who loved them dearly. May the Lord continue to keep each and every one of us as we press toward the mark for the prize of the high calling of God in Christ Jesus (Philippians 3:14). We must continue to run our race until God calls us home. Then, we will see our loved ones again.

≈ *12* ≈

My Life After

After the sentencing of Derrick Todd Lee, I was able to move forward with my life. I continued practicing as a nurse. The other victims' families and I had decided we did not want to attend anymore trials. Our decisions were based on the sentence rendered to Derrick Todd Lee by the judge. He received life for Geralyn DeSoto, and a death sentence for Charlotte Murray Pace. JUSTICE WAS SERVED!

Two years later, as I was working, I experienced a panic attack as my shift was ending for the day. Everything seemed to bombard me all at once. A patient's family member needed to speak with me; the doctor called regarding another patient; two or three patients were requesting meds; and I was trying to complete my paperwork. This situation wasn't unusual for me. I was good at multi-tasking.

But, for some unknown reason, I was unable to organize and address each task. My thought processes became blocked. I felt stuck and unable to carry out any of the tasks required of me. Immediately, I knew something was wrong. I became overwhelmed! I stepped back for a moment and took a deep breath to collect myself. I prayed and asked the Lord for help.

My relief had just clocked in and was ready to receive report from me. Frankly, I felt like a basket case and told him I couldn't handle the job anymore. He asked "Why? What's going on?" I said that the job had become too overwhelming, and I needed to quit.

He encouraged me not to give up. He shared his testimony regarding an oil field accident. While working on an oil rig, he fell from the derrick and shattered both legs. He also suffered a stroke during his recuperation period, which landed him in the nursing home for a certain length of time . . . a few months or a year . . . I don't recall. The Lord healed him from his injuries, and now he was a Licensed

Practical Nurse, caring for the elderly. I was touched by his story. It wasn't evident to see that this man sustained devastating injuries to his legs.

I pondered on the story that I had just heard. I knew in my heart that nobody but the Lord healed him. But, as I reflected on my patients, their well being was important to me. I didn't want to cause harm to any of them by giving the wrong medication or inadequate care. I thanked my relief for the encouragement.

Ultimately, I had to make a sound decision. I went to my supervisor and explained what was happening to me. She understood and asked whether I was certain of my decision. My response was "yes." I thanked her for having me on board as part of the staff. My relief took over from there. I left my job that day and did not return.

While remaining at home, the head pain started all over again. It was constant and excruciating. The episodes were continuous . . . all day long, seven days a week. Nothing relieved it except rest. There were days I wanted to pull my hair out. I sought many doctors to help alleviate my pain. MRIs, CT Scans, and various other tests were done. Different medications were prescribed. Nothing relieved my headaches. So, I spent most of my days resting in a quiet, darkened room, to reduce mental stimulation. Days of bed rest were the only remedy for my situation.

I felt sad for Oliver. He worked and cared for me the best way he knew how. My physical and emotional condition was taking a toll on him and our marriage. I realized I also had unresolved issues. Many of these issues were residuals from my attack. These issues within me were suppressed by staying busy with work, household chores, running errands, and sleep.

I also realized that Oliver and the children needed emotional healing . . . especially Herman. The most unusual thing is that my family and I never discussed the attack. None of my family members, not even my mom or siblings, inquired about the details. I don't know if it was too painful for them to talk about; or perhaps they wanted to spare me from reliving that ordeal again.

There were times I felt the need to talk to Oliver about the attack. For a few seconds during the assault,

I was concerned that my family would come home and find me dead . . . lying in a pool of blood. I saw no way out, because there was no one there to help me . . . except Jesus. I remember telling the Lord that my family would come home and find me dead, and they wouldn't know what happened, or who did it.

It was difficult for me to go to Oliver and talk to him about the things that weighed heavy on my heart. After all, this occurrence affected him also. We were at different levels regarding our needs for healing. The bloody scene was cleaned up by him, our son, Djuanas, and his sister, Linda. I can't begin to imagine their disposition during the clean up process. Therefore, I understood and respected his position.

I came to the realization that I needed counseling. I spoke to my Heavenly Father about what I was going through and asked Him for help. Not long after my talk with the Lord, my beautician, who was also a minister at Destiny of Faith, mentioned a woman on our praise team who was a minister and a professional counselor. I consulted her, and she obligingly took my case.

Minister Debra, the counselor who was on our praise team, came to our home to personally counsel me and Oliver. By the leading of the Holy Spirit, she counseled us individually and as a couple. Her spirit was peaceful, pleasant, and of such great strength. She offered compassion as she explained that I was suffering from Post Traumatic Stress Disorder due to the assault. She handed me a pamphlet that gave definitions and examples of post traumatic stress, and how it affects one's life.

Deep within me laid a problem I had not revealed. When the doorbell rang, or if there was a knock at the door, my body began trembling with fear and my heart rate increased. I did not want to answer the door. Actually, I was really afraid to answer the door. I didn't want anyone to know I was home.

My family had no idea I was struggling with this issue. I did my best to lessen their concerns by not sharing that information with them. I politely asked my family to please call before coming over. The phone calls helped to prepared me for their arrival.

On one occasion, prior to my counseling with

Minister Debra, I experienced a post traumatic moment. Oliver and I were staying in Youngsville, LA., at my sister and her husband's, Dorothy and Eric's, home. Everyone was at work when a white car pulled up in the driveway. I thought it was my sister. The car was identical to hers, including the color. I headed toward the front door to unlock it for her. Before I could reach the door, I saw a Caucasian man with a white shirt knocking at the front door. Immediately, I panicked!

The house had a large window with no curtains. This window was on the front of the house near the front door. The uncovered window provided no privacy from those approaching the front of the house. I was so frightened that I hid down the hall. I did not want this man to know that I was home. I went into the bedroom and watched him through the window until he left. Once he was gone, I came out of the bedroom and sat on the couch in the family room. I was shaken by this stranger knocking at the door. It caused me to relive the day that I opened the door to Derrick Todd Lee. Eventually my heart rated decreased, and I calmed down. I never mentioned the incident to anyone because no one understood what I was going through.

I shared this information with Minister Debra. I also mentioned that I enjoyed walking in the neighborhood but felt uneasy about it. She patiently worked with me and continuously drilled me in walking back and forth to the front door to answer it. She ministered to me and often said, "The Lord really loves you." I would smile and say I love Him too.

These words would penetrate my spirit with a warm comforting feeling. It seemed as though no matter what I was going through, the Lord was reassuring me that He had not forgotten me.

Minister Debra often gave me and Oliver assignments to help improve our communication skills. He and I struggled with the assignments. It wasn't because the assignments were difficult; it was the fact that he and I had emotionally closed the doors to one another due to pain, disappointment, mistrust, and other situations that had taken place in our marriage.

Eventually, I did overcome the anxiety of answering

the door. Walking in the neighborhood was a different matter. With all the senseless things going on in this world, I never got comfortable walking alone in my neighborhood.

The neighborhood wasn't a bad area. Most of the residents worked. I was concerned about someone driving through the neighborhood as I was walking and attacking me or forcing me into a vehicle. I wanted to remain vigilant.

I am so grateful to God for allowing Minister Debra to be a part of our lives. She was a blessing to both of us. To my surprise, Oliver felt comfortable talking to her about issues regarding our marriage, after our lives were shattered from my attack. This was a huge step for him. One of the things Oliver mentioned was that he recognized the emotional dilemma I was going through. He also spoke of the trust issues I had regarding him and that it was putting a strain on our marriage. He said to Minister Debra during counseling that no matter how much he reassures me of his love and commitment to our marriage, I still wavered with the thought of trusting him. The mistrust stemmed from past incidents in our marriage regarding both of us, as well as the head trauma from the assault on my life.

The counseling sessions were coming to an end. Minister Debra gave us positive tools with which to work. Unfortunately, Oliver and I did not apply the different methods we were given by the counselor. We spent most of our time avoiding deep conversations to prevent an argument. We drew further apart until we eventually separated July 2007.

During the separation, the Lord began to show me the areas of my life that needed major adjustments. There was brokenness in many areas of my life that I had not realized. I was sexually assaulted by Derrick Todd Lee, which left me feeling violated and lacking the trust I needed in my own relationship with Oliver.

It was following the separation that God dealt with me regarding my anger and unforgiveness. He revealed to me a spirit of great anger, which was deeply embedded within me, that led me to forgiveness.

During my separation from Oliver, the first thing God taught me was self control. This is one of the fruits of the Spirit in Galatians 5:22. I underwent anger management with the Holy Spirit. I call this the pruning part of my life. There were things within me that the Holy Spirit needed to detach from me, so I could bear good fruit for the Kingdom of God.

Many days were spent in prayer and communicating with the Father. He dissected my life before me in the spiritual realm. There was no denying the truth when God revealed my wretchedness. The innermost thing that was hidden was brought to the forefront. Acknowledging what God had revealed to me was the first step to my deliverance.

The Holy Spirit spoke to my spirit man and said "bitterness." I went to the concordance in back of my Bible and looked up this word. In short, the definition of bitterness states that it is an anger that has settled in for the long term. It is an anger that gives birth to resentment, the feeling that we have been treated harshly, unfairly, and carelessly. It eats deep into our mind, emotions, and even our soul. The poison of bitterness, left unchecked, can destroy us. Three simple words spoken can relieve a lifetime of bitterness—I FORGIVE YOU. WOW! These words summed up what I was experiencing within myself. I was ready for change!

I got down on my knees and began to talk to my Heavenly Father. I thanked Him for revealing to me that very thing that was destroying me from within (bitterness). I repented and asked God to forgive me for sinning against Him. Then I prayed, asking God to forgive me for everyone I intentionally and unintentionally hurt, causing bitterness within them. I asked Him to heal and deliver them from the evil seed of bitterness, which I may have caused. In turn, I told the Lord that I forgive everyone who had intentionally and unintentionally hurt me, including Derrick Todd Lee.

My deliverance came forth and the peace of God rested upon me. I felt free from the burden of bitterness. Today, I can honestly say that, no matter what I go through, I always ask God to guard my heart so anger and bitterness will not take root within me again. These two things will destroy a person from within . . . leaving them with all kinds of health issues.

Forgiveness sets us free, and God's love gives us

PEACE and JOY that is indescribable. This PEACE and JOY is like nothing you've ever known. I can tell you about it, because I live it every day. This does not mean that I have no problems or troubles in this world . . . because I do. The only difference is I talk to God first. Then, I will call my prayer partner, as the Holy Spirit leads me.

Most of all, I try to keep my heart right with God's love that is shed abroad in my heart by the Holy Spirit (Romans 5:5). I do get angry, but again, I try to remember what the Word of God says . . . . "be angry, but sin not" (Ephesians 4:26). His Word also says a kind word turns away wrath (Proverbs 15:1). God is a God of restoration.

≈ *13* ≈

Justice and Restoration

*O*ur lives are precious to the One who created us. It would be wise not to take our lives for granted. My life nearly ended July 9, 2002. Now, I recognize the Power of God and His saving Grace everyday. I don't take my life for granted anymore. I live each day with such spiritual joy that can only come from God. No matter what comes, this joy sustains me as I go through whatever I need to go through. I know the outcome will be good for me, because it builds character and inner strength. Best of all, God rewards me for trusting Him.

God showed Himself REAL on the day of my attack that no judge, lawyer, or juror could ever match. He fought Derrick Todd on my behalf and shielded me from the painful blows delivered.

I sympathize with the families of the women I have written this book in memory of, and for anyone who has experienced a loss or tragedy in their life. There is HOPE! We never forget our loved ones, but Our Heavenly Father gives us the strength to go on. We have our own race to run until God calls us home to be with our loved ones. We must complete the journey, so He can say, "Well done, my good and faithful servant" (Matthew 25:21). The journey is not easy apart from God. We need Him every step of the way.

I thank God for using me to bring Derrick Todd Lee to Justice. This assignment was given to me by my Heavenly Father. He needed me to be the vessel, while He did all the work through me. I don't boost about anything but Jesus Christ. I am nothing without Him. Had it not been for the Holy Spirit living in me and the small still voice that said, *"It's My Will,"* regarding my going forth to testify, I would have done like Jonah . . . gone in the opposite direction of the turmoil. It was God's will for me to come forth, not mine. All Credit, Glory, and Honor, belongs to God. HIS WILL WAS DONE!!!

With God's help, I overcame the internal struggle of bondage called "fear." I was afraid to answer the door, talk to people, and was paranoid in the midst of a crowd. Today, I am free to be who I am and what God has called me to be. I've come to understand that everything happens for a reason; and whatever the reason or purpose may be, there are lessons to learn from each experience. I've learned to depend on God and to trust Him no matter where I find myself in this life. I know He will always come through for me.

God never changes . . . we do. He restores us when we are broken if we let Him. He is a gentleman. He won't pressure us. But, He may use circumstances to draw us to Him. God is good all the time and will be forever and ever. I love Him with all my heart, mind, soul, and body—not because of what He has done for me, but truly, because of WHO HE IS!

Allow Him to fix whatever is broken in your life, or whatever weighs heavy on your heart, mind, and spirit. If you let Jesus have control of your life, no matter what you go through, you won't go through it alone. He'll give you peace in the midst of the storm, while He works everything out for your good. I can *testify* to that, because I AM AN OVERCOMER BY THE BLOOD OF THE LAMB and THE WORD OF MY TESTIMONY (Revelation 12:11).

The End

CPSIA information can be obtained
at www.ICGtesting.com
Printed in the USA
FFOW05n2113090414